A Prescription To Delusion.

Felereen

BookLeaf
Publishing

India | USA | UK

Dedication

To those who resort to writing at any minor inconvenience.

Preface

A Prescription to Delusion is a collection of fictional poems. It entails delusional story telling in the form of poetry. Each poem is a perspective of different characters who are telling their stories in the form of letters but are poems.

Acknowledgements

Thanking God for being generous enough with me, for gifting me writing as my go to therapy.

1. Warm Winter.

Never in my life
Did I listen to the 1975;
But it was that one cold winter,
When my brain was about to wither:
A spark was reignited!
Was it you?
Or was I light hearted?
I suddenly stopped taking things for granted.

You came along with the song,
And took me back to where I belonged.
Never did I think
That you'd be such an awesome thing.

You were as cold as the winter,
And with it,
You brought warmth that lingered
Like chocolate chips and cocoa butter.

I guess you'll never know,
The kind of awakening you had sown,
I guess I'll never show,
How much you made it grow.

I'll never ever mention it,
But in my heart I've stamped it,
As the winter;
The winter I'll never forget.

~ Ember,
University Dorm,
Oslo.
2019.
 "To Aelius, the boy who unconsciously ended her existential crisis."

2. Surreal.

You offer to take a stroll
Instead of making me scroll.
Who are you?
I wish to be told.

The Shillong streets
Have never been this sweet!
We pass by a rookie band,
Playing "Just the way you are."
You're giving me that look,
The kind of look I give
At the sight of a favourite book.

We're now laughing
Over an inside joke,
Now I can't go back
To a time we never spoke.
Why do you have to be such a fine bloke?

We pass by the lake
And petrichor is in our favour;
You know just what to do,
Asking me if I want latte or americano to savour.

This cozy cafe has a zillion books,
Who would have thought that
It has always been your favourite nook?
We're now playing jenga,
While the chef is making your favourite pasta.

We're now under a sea of stars,
Passing by lit up shops,
While I realize that you've become
My Heart throb!

Now I'm wide awake,
Pondering how a simple evening stroll
Could make my dopamine levels go crazy!
I wonder if you're real
Or just someone so surreal!

~ Mabel,
Jaiaw.
2017.
 "To Dashan, the colleague who ended up becoming her
crush."

3. Chamomile Personified.

Zen, isn't it?
It's pouring though,
A sacrificial twist;
What in the world is this?

A calming effect,
That, I did expect.
But not for the chaos
To be perfect!

A low-key shield,
It meant so much to me.
A memory of warmth
Amid the storm.

A mundane day,
Cotton candy feelings,
A grey sky,
Over a mushy pink town.

Ephemeral, isn't it?
Do I need a better boat?
It doesn't do well at docks.
Or do I anchor it into a rock?

You're the epitome of calmness,
A personification of chamomile tea
After the rain.
Well, with you petrichor is a feeling.
Oh, I would love to sink in it.

Dashan,
Sohra.
2017.
 "To Mabel, the girl colleague whom he developed
feelings for. She had always been the calm breeze amid
their chaotic work pressure."

4. Dear Analogy.

You're the sweetest of them all,
Your chivalry
Has become my cup of tea.
I wonder if you think of me
When you see white roses on trees,
The ones we talked about
Over an inevitable afternoon tea.

I see you as charming,
I see you as sweet,
I've never met anyone
Who feels like my favourite book.

You're as green as nature
And that's where I find peace.
You're like the warm breeze
Over the deep black sea,
At night, when all I can do is breathe.

You make my days feel like
Views of sunsets from an airplane.
You exude the kind of strength
That I would feel
When I immerse in the beauty of bright city lights

From the deck of mighty scrapers.

You're my favourite kind of exotic,
With you, I see
New shades of skies, they're majestic,
But the colour of your aura
Is my favourite of all, it is called prolific.

~Valeria,
Aviation School.
2014.
 "To Zeki, the super kind techie neighbour who made the headstrong independent Valeria feel like she's in her soft girl era."

5. Quiet Luxury!

I scribble art,
Whenever I'm left in the dark.
I look for stars,
Oh, I wish it ends at that!

I frame sentences to impress,
Only to make you depressed.
I hate this kind of stress,
But hey, aren't you the best?

Will this remain a secret?
Or be my biggest regret?
Whatever the future may be,
You are now my quiet luxury.

Empathy drives me insane,
Your sympathy is my bane,
I remember you from that lane,
You never changed, you are still the same.

You're unaware of my nonchalant glares
Which are manifestations of adoration!
Oh, to be you;
Admired without having any clue!

~Zeki.

Istanbul.

2018.

"To Valeria, the gorgeous neighbour who Zeki met again after many years in their hometown. He thought it was unrequited love!"

6. Majestic.

Someone's burden is someone's blessing,
I've never met someone so amazing.
You're someone's pure bliss,
You never deserved that diss.
You were madness
Because someone was careless.
Now you're the absolute best.

Someone's exhaustion is someone's exhilaration.
No, it's not a competition.
It's just that your kindness has caught my attention.
Your were not supportive
Because he didn't see you a gift.
Now you're the ultimate gift.

Someone's try is someone's prize.
I surely will have the time of my life!
With you, I shall continue to strive.
I can now be me, not having to seek for sympathy,
We unravel paths as a team,
We embrace peace as lovers,
Oh, with you, I believe in a real and majestic forever.

~Jeremiah.

"To the woman he prayed for, the woman of his
dreams and someone whom he sees as his future wife."

7. Canon in D personified.

I get a glimpse of your smile,
I cannot think straight for a while.
You look extremely nice,
You look charming and wise.

I don't want to be delusional,
But when I look at you,
I hear Canon in D.
I hope this is not extreme.

For you, I couldn't play minor keys,
You are too sweet a tune,
A soothing Melody.
Hoping you won't end up only as a memory.

You're the compass that I'm blessed with beautifully,
The telescope that can make me see
Stars I've never seen.

Please don't ever leave,
Continue to interpret art with me,
Paint my blank canvases
With colourful memories,
Imagine how nice that would be.

~Ruth.

"To Jeremiah, the man who feels too good to be true because heartbreaks in the past traumatized her. She has never met anyone quite like him. She wishes that he stays by her side forever.'

8. Drama.

The charmer in its prime,
Evoking swag in spite of having a jet lag.
Talking to him feels great;
That feeling you feel after completing a long pending
task.
Laughing with him feels like every bite of a Japanese
fluffy cheesecake,
While on a diet!
Oh no, I can't stay quiet.

I hide this crush,
But I can't help but blush;
Oh, this feels like a sugar rush.

I always try to look away,
But I always end up being swayed.
Could you be decent?
With that kind of accent!
I've never seen that kind of swag,
In someone who helps prevent heart attacks.

I wonder if you knew
Or even had a tiny clue
That the day you moved out of town,

I was feeling nothing but blue.

Who would have thought that I'd find you again?
My favourite childhood confidante;
Not as a friend,
But as a silly controversial crush,
Here I am, once again;
This time as your favourite junior resident!

~Iba,
Cardiology Department.
2022
 "To Ethan, the childhood friend who moved out of town years ago. They met again in Delhi and she was flabbergasted when she realised that she was in love with the childhood buddy who would call her Homie."

9. From Him.

Who is this ray of sunshine?
Sometimes she looks like a nerd,
Sometimes she's just absurd.
To my surprise,
She makes me feel at home,
I now pay the price
Of allowing her to call me bro.

She's a playlist of many genres,
Some are my vibe,
Some are out of my league.
She's the reason
I rose back up from my defeat.

I've never seen someone so simple,
Yet so complicated.
She would talk about him,
And I would listen.
I see her as a friend,
To my surprise,
She sometimes makes me nervous.

She would laugh at my jokes
Without any care about perfection,

She thinks that I see her as my homie,
She doesn't realise
That all I see is beauty.
I would see the prettiest pair of eyes
Behind those glasses,
The eyes that roll
When I call her a fake Marxist.
The eyes that radiate so much sunlight on me,
More than I've ever felt in my country of one season.
She's the most beautiful thing I've ever seen.

Will she ever know?
That every time I gave her roses,
In the name of friendship,
Deep down inside,
I wished it was courtship,
Will she ever know?
That whenever we danced in the name of friendship,
All she did was
Took my breath away.

She is still a sweet friend to me,
To my surprise,
The only one I can rely on to eternity.
But, she's now far away from me,
Living her dreams
In her dream country.

~Ethan,

AIIMS.

2024.

"To Iba, the girl he was always in love with. In fact, this love blossomed since their childhood days. She was his first crush! He was shattered when he moved out of town. When they met again, he never had the guts to confess, she was too important to lose."

10. Tinge of Sadness.

It's been a year, isn't it?
I may have healed,
Very much far from crying,
But sometimes when I sing,
I can't deny that it still stings.

I can't help but wonder,
If bookstores and and libraries
Remind you of me?"
Or if I cross your mind,
Every time you hear a Taylor Swift song,
I know it has been quite long,
But not long enough to forget my favourite song.

Or does your mind go into a tailspin
Every time you see a Claude Monet's painting.
Do you remember how you painted my days with bright colours
And then changed your palette to darker hues,
Until the background gave off the most chaotic view.

Do you still savour pasta
After all that fiesta?
Or does the word Alfredo

Make you choke a little,
And makes you reflect on your fresco.

I wonder if bright city lights
Make your head feel dizzy
Cause New York was my dream
And you told me that it was my identity.

I wonder if you still smile
When you see inside jokes around the city,
The ones invented by me
Over evening strolls and cheese cake ice cream.

Or what if you feel nothing?
Even when you pass by that mural
You didn't discard.
And What if I'm just a past
Not linked with any sort of feeling?
What if this is just my thing?
Because after all, you never bought me a ring.

~Mabel.
2022.
 "To Dashan, a year after their heart shattering breakup.
They had four glorious years together but some things
are just not meant to be."

11. Splash of Sadness.

My disappearance
Was your deliverance.
It was rough for me
But it surely made you tough.
Now you're living your dreams
While I weep and suppress screams.

You're now living in your right time,
But you're no longer mine,
Yet I struggled with you;
When you weren't fine.
You can now buy her peace,
For She wouldn't have any reason to leave.
You can now freely breathe
While all she can do is gleam.

My patience did pay off,
You're now pretty well off.
But, you're better off
Without me;
Who is roaming around Paris
Contemplating about the transaction of promises.

~Iba.

Paris.

2023.

 "To her ex-boyfriend, the guy she would tell Ethan about."

12. Melancholy.

I miss his melancholic eyes,
They had probably seen
Our future goodbyes.

I miss his humour,
He probably made me laugh enough
To help me embrace my mundane future.

I miss his gentle voice,
Contrary to the brutal reality
He left me with,
A reality where I had no choice!

~Mabel.
2022.
 "To Dashan."

13. Unsung Hero.

You were the invisible source of joy,
The invisible source of strength.
I wonder if you'll ever know,
That you helped me get to great lengths.

Memories you are memories of blurry city lights,
On cold winter nights.
You encouraged me
And shed on some light.

I never imagined that you'd leave a void,
One that doesn't make me paranoid.
You left me with a warm and fuzzy kind of nostalgia,
Imbued with a bit of longing and a bit of reminiscing,
Oh, how I miss your singing!

Wherever you are, you've set the bar so high,
Notwithstanding being separated by the Pacific or the
Atlantic,
In my heart you shall always be
The most prolific in being heroic.

~Iba.
New York, relocated.

2024.

"To Ethan, the unsung hero who was always there for her during her darkest phase, notwithstanding the time or distance, he made sure to help her heal."

14. Sapphire.

Sapphires are cold and blue,
And so are you.
I bet sapphires don't know their worth
The same way you never did since birth.

Some things are meant to sparkle,
But only for others to see.
Does it not sound like a debacle?
But no, that's how it's ought to be.

Though others couldn't interfere
Regarding how you feel,
They somehow should be grateful
To have you as their shield.

I think sapphires are humble,
They do not see their lustre,
But that's okay,
They do make others feel better.

You are a gem,
Maybe someday you'll know.
But even if you don't,
You'll still shine like a sapphire,

And would always win through trials by fire.

~Ethan,
New York.
2025.
 "To Iba, on the fourteenth of February, 2025. He confessed. She was thrilled. They are now dating. Who would have thought? But, as the old saying goes, 'What's meant for you will always be yours.' Their cute story ends here but their happily ever after begins in real life."

15. An old teen.

Never been this smitten,
Silly fainting in my room
Replaying your cheeky smiles in my mind.
Oh damn, I'm losing my mind.

Don't look at me with those hazel brown eyes,
They already omitted the word delusional from my
dictionary.

Don't laugh at my off kilter banters,
I melt.
Damn, I bet!
Now, I'm secretly obsessed.

Don't call me funny,
Because that's when I say goodbye to rationality.
Okay, this is scary,
I'm no longer a teen,
But these butterflies are definitely taking over my
dreams.

~Aurora.
28 years old.
      "To her Publisher, the guy who makes her feel

like a teenager all over again. She is apprehensive as well as excited."

16. Fluency.

It is funny how
I need not ask about what you like,
I just know it!

Your eyes glimmer as though they reflect a starry sky,
Your mind exudes calmness
As though you love nature.

Your strength shows that you've been through hell and
back
And now support those who lack.

You're a wild thing;
Wild that I know you too well
Without you having to say anything.

Not asking you questions makes me bold,
Because surprisingly, I am fluent in the language of your
soul.

This may be a point of soul crossings,
A momentary bliss before diverging.
To get my daily dose of sunshine,
To feel warmth in the rain, come what may.

To love the process without being obsessed,
To embrace prayers for you,
Keeping in mind that you're the best.

You could have been sent only for this point in my life,
But how I wish,
That it would stay this way:
Tomorrow, the year after or maybe forever.

I don't want you to be a phase
Because I know you'd brighten up all my days.
For as long as I live,
I want you to be mine,
To care, to cherish
And to have the time of our lives.

I've never written a love poem
With tears in my eyes,
Fire in my soul
And warmth in my heart;
I can't even call you the one
Because I can't be too sure.

But I'm writing this with zeal
And passion,
Away from all distractions,
Soaking up in my mushy feelings,

Pondering if this is just some crazy attraction.

Amid all this, I know one thing is true,
And that is:
I won't be able to trust myself
If I ever fall in love with you.

~Aurora's Publisher.

   "To Aurora, a unique woman who intrigues him so much to a point where he is ready to cross the line of professionalism. He feels like he understands the language of her soul."

17. Warmth.

For someone whose forte is thinking,
Never did it cross my mind
That I would one day personify warmth.
I thought I'd have it together by 25,
Well, here I am,
Only being mesmerized by your eyes.

I see your path being parallel to mine,
But what's this enduring urge to hop onto your line?
I never knew that if warmth could talk,
The heart would go berserk.

It's human nature to seek for that shine and light,
And I end up looking forward to your smiles so bright.
To know warmth
Is to know debates between your heart and mind.
He makes me feel warm
But, what if in reality I'm only inviting a storm?

It's sad to say I want you so much,
But I don't think these parallel lines would ever touch.
You may not know how much I care,
But I love it when I get those charming glares.

You may have crossed my path
To take me out of the dark,
We may tread different roads
But you're one of the best people I've never known,
I shall carry this feeling with me down the road,
And I guess you'll never know!

~Hana.
PhD. Scholar, Department of Biomedical Engineering
 NUS.
 "To Kai, her karate instructor, who seem like a playboy,
looks like a South Korean model and actor. She looks
forward to her Karate classes amid her academic
pressure."

18. Rare.

I like the calmness
When I'm around you.
I've experienced butterflies
And sped up lubb dubb sounds,
But, now I'm shook
By the sound of peace.
Not that I ever thought I'd hear its sound,
But that's the only thing that resounds
When you're around.

I needed the sun for cortisol,
But then I met your ethereal eyes
And now they calm my soul.
I wonder what I'm going through,
Being drawn to someone's beautiful soul.
This attraction is rare,
Damn it, I caught feelings!
It was always nice talking to you,
But now I'm listening to songs
And you're crossing my mind.
Oh dear, now I have to bear the brunt
Of liking someone.

~Hana,

"To Kai. OOPS!!!! SHE CAUGHT FEELINGS!!!"

19. Nonchalant.

Will you ever know that I write poems for you?
You seem nonchalant
But I'm so mesmerized by you.
You do seem to know art,
But you're still left in the dark,
You ignite within me a certain kind of spark.

I notice silly things about you,
And damn, you're gorgeous too!
I wonder if you see me too,
In ways I think of you.

You could be pretty chatty,
But you could just be someone friendly,
I'm too old for unrequited love,
But damn those eyes, they're pretty tough.

Sometimes I think you play along,
Pretending to like my kind of songs,
But I could also be wrong,
What if our bond is actually strong?

I am in love with your smirks,
But what if it means that you're a jerk?

Being exposed to those smiles feels like a perk,
I think I need to focus on my work.

I sometimes think I am insane,
Well, my days are not mundane,
You could end up being a bane,
But at least, you'll dance with me in the rain.

~Hana.
 "To Kai. Her feelings grew!"

20. Risk.

I want to try this with you
But you're too addictive to lose.
Being loved by you would be cute
But I am not risking the aftermath
I might seriously go mad.

You seem like a bad boy,
But why are you so coy?
I do not want to destroy
Whatever this is, it gives me joy.

If I take this path,
You'd be my wildest risk,
We'd be dancing in the mist,
And be in a cheerful bliss!

But this is all delusional,
I need to be practical,
Someone needs to pop this bubble,
So I would not get into trouble!

~Hana.
"To Kai, her biggest crush. This what we call opposites
attract because Kai seems to be mesmerized by nerdy

Hana a lot and Hana seems to be deviating a lot, in fact, QUITE A LOT, from her usual type. She does not understand how they vibe with each other but only one thing keeps her going, "He brightens up her mundane days."

21. Situational Comedy.

So now there's a distance,
In just an instant.
I do not want to be blatant,
But I can't live under this delusion.

Are you nervous?
Or am I being dismissed?
Is it her?
Oh, damn this dreamer!

I knew you were a risk,
A temporary bliss.
I wouldn't call this a heartbreak,
More so, should I even rage?

I'm not even your type, am I?
But you've grown on me
Like my favourite series,
And now I'm halfway through
This cute situational comedy,
Not realizing that even they have finales.

But barring all that negativity,
You did colour my colourless season,

So, for some reason,
I'll never regret this.

~Hana.
 "Well, he is exactly who she thought he was. The thing
is that Hannah saw all the red flags but she decided to be
colourblind for him,"